Essential COOKING SERIES
COMPREHENSIVE, STEP BY STEP COOKING
Baking

BUDGET
BOOKS

Food Editor: Jody Vassallo
Project Editor: Lara Morcombe
Design: Studio Pazzo
Cover Design: Budget Books

Essential Cooking Series: Baking
This edition first published in 2008 by Budget Books
45–55 Fairchild Street
Heatherton, Victoria, 3202, Australia
www.hinklerbooks.com

10 9 8
13 12 11 10 09

© Text and Design Hinkler Books Pty Ltd
© Step-by-Step Shots and Hero Shots on pages
12–13, 15, 16–17, 25, 28–29, 32, 33, 36–37, 40–41, 42–43, 52–53, 54–55, 56–57
Hinkler Books Pty Ltd
© Hero Shots on pages 8–9, 10-11, 14, 18-19, 20–21, 22-23, 24, 26–27, 30–31,
34–35, 38, 39, 44–45, 46, 47, 48–49, 50–51
R&R Publications licensed to Hinkler Books Pty Ltd

Disclaimer: The nutritional information listed under each recipe does not
include the nutrient content of garnishes or any accompaniments not listed
in specific quantitites in the ingredient list. The nutritional information for
each recipe is an estimate only, and may vary depending on the brand of
ingredients used, and due to natural biological variations in the composition
of natural foods such as meat, fish, fruit and vegetables. The nutritional
information was calculated by using Foodworks dietary analysis software
(Version 3, Xyris Software Pty Ltd, Highgate Hill, Queensland, Australia) based
on the Australian food composition tables and food manufacturers' data.
Where not specified, ingredients are always analysed as average or medium,
not small or large.

ISBN: 978 1 7412 1937 1

Printed and bound in China

Contents

An introduction to baking

Oat-bran fruit muffins offer a fresh interpretation of a classic breakfast, lemon currant muffins are perfect with a cup of warm tea, and blue cheese and walnut damper adds a rustic touch to a dinner party menu. Quick breads range from muffins, scones and hot cross buns to croissants, banana bread and damper. What they all have in common is that they are cooked without yeast, they rarely require kneading and they are quick and easy to make.

QUICK BREADS

The whole process of making quick breads can take less time than it would for you to jump into a car and shop for pre-made breads at your local supermarket. It can be as simple as sifting together a few dry ingredients, whisking some eggs, butter and liquid, gently combining the lot, pouring the batter into muffin pans, whacking it in the oven and waiting until cooked.

Quick breads can be cooked in muffin tins, on baking trays or in loaf tins. The size of the loaf tin will not make that much difference. If the tin is larger than the one suggested in the recipe, the cooking time will be shorter. Take care, however, not to try to cook it in a smaller tin as the bread needs room to rise and if the tin is too small the

batter will spill over the side of the tin. Cook quick breads until a skewer inserted into the centre comes out clean. There are three main methods for preparing quick bread mixtures:

1   Muffin method.

2   Scone method – which involves rubbing cold butter into the dry ingredients until the mixture resembles coarse breadcrumbs before stirring in the liquid and mixing it to form a soft dough.

3   Creaming method – beating butter and sugar with electric beaters until light and fluffy, then gradually adding the eggs, followed by a portion of the dry ingredients folded in with a portion of the liquid ingredients. The creaming method produces a finer more cake-like textured quick bread as the emphasis is on adding air to the mixture.

MUFFINS

First thing you will need to do before you start is to preheat your oven. Muffins are usually cooked on a slightly higher temperature than cakes so check the recipe, but as a rough guide it is likely you will be cooking at 200°C (400°F, gas mark 6).

Check the recommended tin size. Don't panic if you do not have the exact size – this usually means that you will end up with more or less muffins. Non-stick muffin tins come in a variety of sizes. The most popular are: 1 cup (Texas muffin) tin with 6 holes; $1/2$ cup tin with 12 holes; $1/3$ cup tin with 12 holes; and mini muffin tins with 12 holes. The easiest way to measure the capacity of a tin is to measure out 1 cup (250 ml, 8 fl oz) water in a jug and pour it into a hole until it reaches the top. If you are planning to line the holes with paper cases do this before you start preparing the mixture. If the paper cases are thin you may want to use a double layer to help them sit in place.

Now it is time to read the recipe and measure out the ingredients. Sift the flour and dry ingredients into a large bowl that has enough room for the ingredients to be mixed together without spilling any over the side. Make a well in the centre of the dry ingredients; this will give you a place into which you can pour the liquid ingredients. Set this bowl aside while you whisk together the wet mixture. This is best done in a jug as it makes pouring easier. Whisk the ingredients together either with a small whisk or fork until well combined – this is quite important as they are only gently stirred through the dry ingredients and unbeaten egg can be a problem.

Now pour all of the liquid into the well and fold them together using either a large spatula or metal spoon. It is very important not to over mix the batter – it should still be quite lumpy. If you over beat a muffin batter you will find yourself with bouncy rubbery muffins rather than lightly textured moist ones. Spoon the mixture into the prepared holes, only fill the holes to three quarters full as muffins need room to rise and peak at the top.

Place the muffins on the middle shelf of the preheated oven. Cook for the specified recipe time but check about 5 minutes before the end of cooking as fan-forced ovens can be hotter and cook faster than normal convection ovens. You may also need to turn the tin during cooking if the back of your oven is hotter than the front.

There are a couple of ways to test whether a muffin is cooked. Often you will be able to see that the muffin has started to come away from the side of the tin. Otherwise, insert a skewer into the centre of the muffin and if it comes out clean it is cooked.

Allow the muffins to cool in the tin for about 5 minutes before turning out onto a wire rack to cool completely or eat warm with some butter and a cup of coffee.

Basic sweet muffin recipe
300 g (10 oz) self-raising flour
125 g (4 oz) castor sugar
1 1/2 cups (375 ml, 12 fl oz) buttermilk
2 eggs
150 g (5 oz) butter, melted and cooled
  slightly

1 Preheat oven to 200°C (400°F, gas mark 6). Sift flour into a bowl and stir in sugar. Make a well in the centre.

2 Whisk together the buttermilk, eggs and butter. Pour into the dry ingredients and mix gently until the mixture is just combined.

3 Spoon the mixture into 12 of the 1/2-cup capacity muffins holes and bake for 20–25 minutes or until risen and golden and starting to come away from the side of the tin.

Note: For a basic savoury muffin recipe, delete the sugar.

Storage
Cooled cooked muffins can be stored at room temperature in an air-tight container for 2–3 days. Frozen muffins can be stored in plastic wrap or a freezer bag for up to 3 months. Thaw at room temperature or in the microwave on defrost.

SCONES

There are a couple of simple tips that will help you when making scones. Firstly, use cold butter to rub into the flour. You can either cut the butter into the flour using a flat bladed knife or you can rub the butter in using your fingertips. Whatever you decide, work quickly.

Make a well in the centre and pour in the liquid. Mix the ingredients together using a flat bladed knife; the mixture should come together in clumps. Remember it is better to add liquid to the mixture rather than flour. Gather the dough together with your hands and turn it out on a lightly floured surface.

Scones should not be kneaded, as this will make the dough tough and heavy. Pat or roll out the dough and use a lightly floured cutter to remove rounds of the dough. Place the scones close, but not touching, onto a baking tray lined with baking paper or lightly greased. Brush the tops with milk as this gives them a golden top as they bake.

Checking scones for readiness is tricky. Probably the best way is to break a scone open to see if it is light and fluffy inside. If it is still moist and slightly wet, cook the scones for a little longer.

If you prefer soft topped scones to those with a crisper top, wrap the warm scones in a clean tea towel and allow them to cool slightly.

Cheddar and pepper muffins

INGREDIENTS

250 g (8 oz) plain flour
1½ teaspoons baking powder
½ teaspoon bicarbonate of soda
½ teaspoon salt
¼ teaspoon cayenne pepper
90 g (3 oz) polenta
250 g (8 oz) mature cheddar, grated
6–8 spring onions (green onions),
    green tops sliced thinly
1 small red capsicum (pepper), diced
4 tablespoons butter
2 tablespoons sugar
2 eggs
1¼ cups (315 ml, 10 fl oz) buttermilk
makes 18

PREPARATION TIME
20 minutes

COOKING TIME
20 minutes

1 Preheat oven to 220°C (425°F, gas mark 7). Into a large bowl, sift flour, baking powder, bicarbonate of soda, salt and cayenne pepper. Add polenta, cheddar, spring onions and capsicum and mix to combine.

2 In a separate large bowl, beat butter and sugar until creamy, add eggs and beat until smooth. Fold dry ingredients into butter mixture alternately with buttermilk until just combined.

3 Spoon batter into 18 greased ⅓ cup (80 ml, 2¾ fl oz) capacity muffin tins and bake for 15–18 minutes or until muffins are cooked when tested with a skewer. Turn onto wire racks to cool.

NUTRITIONAL VALUE PER SERVE	FAT **12.7** G	CARBOHYDRATE **23** G	PROTEIN **9.5** G

Mushroom muffins

INGREDIENTS

250 g (8 oz) plain flour
1 tablespoon baking powder
60 g (2 oz) mushrooms, chopped
110 g (3½oz) brown rice
60 g (2 oz) mature cheddar, grated
1 tablespoon dried parsley
2 teaspoons chopped fresh chives
125 g (4 oz) butter, melted
1 cup (250 ml, 8 fl oz) milk
1 egg, beaten
makes 12

PREPARATION TIME
25 minutes

COOKING TIME
12–15 minutes

1 Preheat oven to 200°C (400°F, gas mark 6). Into a large bowl, sift
   flour and baking powder. Add mushrooms, rice, cheese, parsley and
   chives and mix to combine.

2 Make a well in the centre. Add the butter, milk and egg and mix
   until just combined.

3 Spoon mixture into lightly greased ½ cup (125 ml, 4 fl oz) capacity
   muffin tins and bake for 12–15 minutes or until muffins are cooked
   when tested with a skewer. Turn onto wire racks to cool.

| NUTRITIONAL VALUE PER SERVE | FAT 15.1 G | CARBOHYDRATE 31 G | PROTEIN 7.5 G |

Tuscan herb muffins

INGREDIENTS

250 g (8 oz) unbleached plain flour
1 tablespoon baking powder
1 teaspoon bicarbonate of soda
½ teaspoon salt
1 teaspoon dried oregano
1 teaspoon dried thyme
1 teaspoon dried basil
2 eggs
1 egg white
1 cup (250 ml, 8 fl oz) buttermilk
4 tablespoons olive oil
1 tablespoon honey
2 tablespoons grated parmesan
makes 12

PREPARATION TIME
20 minutes

COOKING TIME
25 minutes

1 Preheat oven to 200°C (400°F, gas mark 6). In a large bowl, combine flour, baking powder, bicarbonate of soda, salt, oregano, thyme and basil. Set aside.

2 In a separate large bowl, combine eggs, egg white, buttermilk, oil, honey and parmesan. Pour egg mixture into flour mixture, stirring until just combined.

3 Pour mixture into 12 greased ½ cup (125 ml, 4 fl oz) capacity muffin tins and bake for 20–25 minutes or until muffins are cooked when tested with a skewer. Turn onto wire racks to cool.

NUTRITIONAL VALUE PER SERVE	FAT 12.5 G	CARBOHYDRATE 30 G	PROTEIN 7.6 G

Potato sour cream muffins

INGREDIENTS

250 g (8 oz) mashed potato
2 eggs, lightly beaten
1 cup (250 ml, 8 fl oz) milk
3/4 cup (185 ml, 6 fl oz) sour cream
4 tablespoons butter, melted
315 g (10 oz) self-raising flour, sifted
3 tablespoons snipped fresh chives
makes 6

1 Preheat oven to 180°C (350°F, gas mark 4). In a large bowl, combine potatoes, eggs, milk, sour cream and butter.

2 In a separate bowl, combine flour and chives. Add to potato mixture and mix until just combined. Spoon mixture into 6 greased 1 cup (250 ml, 8 fl oz) capacity muffin tins and bake for 25–30 minutes or until muffins are cooked when tested with a skewer. Turn onto wire racks to cool.

PREPARATION TIME
15 minutes

COOKING TIME
30 minutes

NUTRITIONAL VALUE PER SERVE FAT **11.2** G CARBOHYDRATE **24** G PROTEIN **5.5** G

Cheesy apple muffins

INGREDIENTS

185 g (6 oz) wholemeal
  self-raising flour
¼ teaspoon ground cinnamon
¼ teaspoon ground nutmeg
¼ teaspoon ground ginger
¼ teaspoon ground cloves
1 teaspoon baking powder
45 g (1½ oz) oat bran
3 tablespoons brown sugar
1 green apple, peeled and grated
125 g (4 oz) ricotta
2 tablespoons vegetable oil
¾ cup (185 ml, 6 fl oz) apple juice
makes 12

1 Preheat oven to 200°C (400°F, gas mark 6). Into a large bowl, sift flour, cinnamon, nutmeg, ginger, cloves and baking powder. Add oat bran and sugar, mix to combine.

2 Make a well in the centre of the flour mixture. Stir in apple, ricotta, oil and apple juice and mix until just combined.

3 Spoon mixture into lightly greased ½ cup (125 ml, 4 fl oz) capacity muffin tins. Bake for 25 minutes or until muffins are cooked when tested with a skewer. Turn onto wire racks to cool.

PREPARATION TIME
10 minutes

COOKING TIME
25 minutes

NUTRITIONAL VALUE PER SERVE	FAT 7.3 G	CARBOHYDRATE 26 G	PROTEIN 5.5 G

Pumpkin muffins

INGREDIENTS

165 g (5½ oz) plain flour
100 g (3½ oz) buckwheat flour
½ cup (125 g, 4 oz) sugar
1½ teaspoons baking powder
1 teaspoon ground cinnamon
½ teaspoon bicarbonate of soda
½ teaspoon salt
2 eggs, slightly beaten
250 g (8 oz) pumpkin,
  cooked and mashed
½ cup (125 ml, 4 fl oz) low-fat milk
2 tablespoons cooking oil
½ teaspoon grated orange
  rind (zest)
4 tablespoons orange juice
extra butter for greasing
makes 12

PREPARATION TIME
15 minutes

COOKING TIME
15-20 minutes

1 Preheat oven to 200°C (400°F, gas mark 6). In a large bowl, combine flour, buckwheat flour, sugar, baking powder, cinnamon, bicarbonate of soda and salt. Make a well in the centre of flour mixture and set aside.

2 In a separate bowl, combine eggs, pumpkin, milk, oil, orange rind and orange juice. Add to the flour mixture and mix until just combined.

3 Spoon batter into 12 greased ½ cup (125 ml, 4 fl oz) capacity muffin tins. Bake for 15–20 minutes or until cooked when tested with a skewer. Cool in tins for 5 minutes. Transfer onto a wire rack to cool.

NUTRITIONAL VALUE PER SERVE	FAT 5.3 G	CARBOHYDRATE 32 G	PROTEIN 5.6 G

Mango bran muffins

INGREDIENTS

125 g (4 oz) self-raising flour
2 teaspoons baking powder
1 teaspoon ground cardamom
45 g (1½ oz) oat bran
4 tablespoons brown sugar
1 mango, chopped
2 egg whites
¾ cup (185 ml, 6 fl oz) low-fat milk
4 tablespoons vegetable oil
makes 12

PREPARATION TIME
15 minutes

COOKING TIME
20 minutes

1 Preheat oven to 190°C (375°F, gas mark 5). Into a large bowl, sift flour, baking powder and cardamom. Add bran, sugar and mango and mix to combine.

2 In a large bowl, place egg whites, milk and oil and whisk to combine. Stir milk mixture into flour mixture and mix well to combine.

3 Spoon mixture into 12 nonstick ½ cup (125 ml, 4 fl oz) capacity muffin tins and bake for 15–20 minutes or until muffins are cooked when tested with a skewer. Turn onto a wire rack to cool.

NUTRITIONAL VALUE PER SERVE	FAT **10.3** G	CARBOHYDRATE **26** G	PROTEIN **5** G

Spiced apple muffins

INGREDIENTS

200 g (7 oz) plain wholemeal flour
1 tablespoon baking powder
1 teaspoon ground mixed spice
pinch of salt
4 tablespoons brown sugar
1 medium egg, beaten
220 ml (7½ fl oz) low-fat milk
4 tablespoons butter
1 cooking apple, peeled,
   cored and chopped
makes 9

PREPARATION TIME
20 minutes

COOKING TIME
20 minutes

1 Preheat oven to 200°C (400°F, gas mark 6). Line a muffin or deep bun tin with 9 muffin cases and set aside. In a large bowl, combine flour, baking powder, mixed spice and salt.

2 In another large bowl, combine sugar, egg, milk and melted butter. Gently fold in the flour mixture until just combined – do not over handle. The mixture should be quite lumpy. Gently fold in apple.

3 Divide mixture between the muffin cases. Bake in the oven for 20 minutes or until cooked when tested with a skewer. Transfer to a wire rack to cool.

| NUTRITIONAL VALUE PER SERVE | FAT 9.1 G | CARBOHYDRATE 29 G | PROTEIN 6 G |

Choc rough muffins

INGREDIENTS

125 g (4 oz) sugar
½ cup (125 g, 4 oz) sugar
2 eggs, lightly beaten
250 g (8 oz) self-raising flour, sifted
4 tablespoons cocoa powder, sifted
175 g (5½ oz) chocolate chips
45 g (1½ oz) desiccated coconut
¾ cup (185 ml, 6 fl oz) buttermilk
   or milk
makes 6

PREPARATION TIME
15 minutes

COOKING TIME
35 minutes

1 Preheat oven to 180°C (350°F, gas mark 4). In a large bowl, place butter and sugar and beat until light and fluffy. Gradually beat in eggs.

2 In a separate bowl, combine flour and cocoa powder. Add flour mixture, chocolate chips, coconut and milk to butter mixture and mix until just combined.

3 Spoon mixture into 6 greased 1 cup (250 ml, 8 fl oz) capacity muffin tins and bake for 35 minutes or until muffins are cooked when tested with a skewer. Turn onto wire racks to cool.

NUTRITIONAL VALUE PER SERVE	FAT **19.4** G	CARBOHYDRATE **40** G	PROTEIN **6.7** G

Oat-bran fruit muffins

INGREDIENTS

185 g (6 oz) self-raising flour
75 g (2½ oz) oat bran
95 g (3 oz) brown sugar
½ cup (125 ml, 4 fl oz) vegetable oil
2 eggs
85 g (3 oz) dried mixed fruit,
   chopped
1 cup (250 ml, 8 fl oz) buttermilk
makes 12

1 Preheat oven to 190°C (375°F, gas mark 5).
   In a large bowl, combine flour, oat bran and
   brown sugar.

2 In a separate bowl, whisk together oil and
   eggs and add to the dry ingredients. Add dried
   mixed fruit and buttermilk and mix until just
   combined.

3 Spoon mixture into lightly greased ½ cup
   (125 ml, 4 fl oz) capacity muffin tins. Bake for
   25–30 minutes until muffins are cooked when
   tested with a skewer. Turn onto wire racks
   to cool.

PREPARATION TIME
15 minutes

COOKING TIME
30 minutes

NUTRITIONAL VALUE PER SERVE   FAT **15.7** G   CARBOHYDRATE **35** G   PROTEIN **5.9** G

Banana choc-chip muffins

INGREDIENTS

1 large ripe banana, mashed
1 cup (250 ml, 8 fl oz) milk
1 egg
125 g (4 oz) butter, melted
185 g (6 oz) self-raising flour
125 g (4 oz) castor sugar
130 g (4½ oz) choc bits
makes 12

1 Preheat oven to 190°C (375°F, gas mark 5).
   In a large bowl, combine banana, milk, egg
   and melted butter. Add flour, sugar and choc
   bits and mix until just combined.

2 Spoon mixture into well-greased ½ cup
   (125 ml, 4 fl oz) capacity muffin tins. Bake for
   20 minutes or until muffins are cooked when
   tested with a skewer. Turn onto wire racks to
   cool.

PREPARATION TIME
15 minutes

COOKING TIME
20 minutes

NUTRITIONAL VALUE PER SERVE   FAT **15.3** G   CARBOHYDRATE **38** G   PROTEIN **4.8** G

Sticky date muffins

INGREDIENTS

250 g (8 oz) self-raising flour
1 teaspoon bicarbonate of soda
1 teaspoon ground cinnamon
4 tablespoons brown sugar
90 g (3 oz) butter
125 g (4 oz) pitted dates, chopped
1 egg, lightly beaten
1 cup (250 ml, 8 fl oz) buttermilk
  or milk
brandy sauce
100 g (3¹/₂ oz) butter
3 tablespoons brown sugar
1 tablespoon golden syrup
1 tablespoon brandy
makes 6

PREPARATION TIME
20 minutes

COOKING TIME
35 minutes

1 Preheat oven to 190°C (375°F, gas mark 5). Into a large bowl, sift flour, bicarbonate of soda and cinnamon. Set aside.

2 Place 4 tablespoons sugar, 90 g (3 oz) butter and dates in a small pan and heat over a low heat, stirring constantly until butter melts. Pour date mixture into dry ingredients, add egg and milk. Mix until just combined.

3 Spoon mixture into 6 greased 1 cup (250 ml, 8 fl oz) capacity muffin tins and bake for 30 minutes until muffins are cooked when tested with a skewer.

4 Place remaining butter and sugar, golden syrup and brandy in a small pan and heat over a low heat, stirring constantly, until sugar dissolves. Bring to the boil, reduce heat and simmer for 3 minutes until sauce is thick and syrupy. Serve with warm muffins.

NUTRITIONAL VALUE PER SERVE	FAT **16.2** G	CARBOHYDRATE **40** G	PROTEIN **4** G

Orange-raisin muffins

INGREDIENTS

250 g (8 oz) unbleached plain flour
125 g (4 oz) sugar
1 tablespoon baking powder
1/2 teaspoon salt
60 g (2 oz) raisins
1 egg
1 cup (250 ml, 8 fl oz) milk
3 tablespoons butter, melted
2 teaspoons grated orange
    rind (zest)
makes 12

PREPARATION TIME
15 minutes

COOKING TIME
25 minutes

1 Preheat oven to 200°C (400°F, gas mark 6). In a large bowl,
    combine flour, sugar, baking powder, salt, and raisins. Make a well
    in the centre.

2 In a medium bowl, beat egg, milk, melted butter and orange rind.
    Add egg mixture to flour mixture, stirring until just combined.

3 Spoon mixture into 12 greased 1/2 cup (125 ml, 4 fl oz) capacity
    muffin tins. Bake for 20–25 minutes or until muffins are cooked
    when tested with a skewer. Turn onto wire racks to cool.

NUTRITIONAL VALUE PER SERVE	FAT 8 G	CARBOHYDRATE 44 G	PROTEIN 5.4 G

Mini chocolate muffins with mocha sauce

INGREDIENTS

60 g (2 oz) unsalted butter, diced,
  plus extra for greasing
60 g (2 oz) plain cooking chocolate,
  roughly chopped
2 medium eggs
100 g (3½ oz) castor sugar
100 g (3½ oz) self-raising flour
30 g (1 oz) cocoa powder, sifted,
  plus extra for dusting
mocha sauce
150 g (5o z) plain chocolate, roughly
  chopped
90 mL (3 fl oz) espresso or other
  strong, good quality coffee
155 mL (5o z) double cream
makes 12

1 Preheat oven to 180°C (350°F, gas mark 4). Melt chocolate and butter in a bowl set over a pan of simmering water. In a large bowl, place the eggs, sugar, flour and cocoa powder. Beat for 1 minute then fold in melted chocolate and butter.

2 Spoon batter into 12 greased ½ cup (125 ml, 4 fl oz) capacity muffin tins. Bake for 15 minutes or until muffins are cooked when tested with a skewer. Turn onto wire racks to cool.

3 Place the chocolate, coffee and 4 tablespoons of the cream into a small pan and heat gently. Simmer for 1–2 minutes, until sauce has thickened slightly. Keep warm.

4 Allow muffins to cool on a wire rack for 5 minutes. Whisk remaining cream until thickened, spoon over the muffins along with the mocha sauce. Serve dusted with cocoa powder.

PREPARATION TIME
20 minutes

COOKING TIME
25 minutes

| NUTRITIONAL VALUE PER SERVE | FAT 23.9 G | CARBOHYDRATE 36 G | PROTEIN 5.8 G |

Banana and pineapple muffins

INGREDIENTS

185 g (6 oz) wholemeal
 self-raising flour
1 teaspoon baking powder
1 teaspoon mixed spice
4 tablespoons brown sugar
45 g (1½ oz) oat bran
1 small banana, mashed
150 g (5 oz) can crushed
 pineapple, drained
3 egg whites, lightly beaten
2 tablespoons vegetable oil
½ cup (125 ml, 4 fl oz) pineapple juice
makes 12

1 Preheat oven to 200°C (400°F, gas mark 6).
 Into a large bowl, sift flour, baking powder
 and spice. Add sugar and oat bran and mix
 to combine.

2 Make a well in the centre of the flour mixture.
 In a separate bowl, combine banana, pineapple,
 egg whites, oil and juice. Stir into flour mixture
 and mix until just combined.

3 Spoon mixture into lightly greased ½ cup
 (125 ml, 4 fl oz) capacity muffin tins. Bake for
 12–15 minutes or until muffins are cooked
 when tested with a skewer. Turn onto wire
 racks to cool.

PREPARATION TIME
20 minutes

COOKING TIME
20 minutes

NUTRITIONAL VALUE PER SERVE	FAT 5.7 G	CARBOHYDRATE 30 G	PROTEIN 5.6 G

Carrot ginger muffins

INGREDIENTS

250 g (8 oz) unbleached plain flour
1 tablespoon baking powder
1 teaspoon bicarbonate of soda
1/2 teaspoon salt
1/2 teaspoon ground nutmeg
1/2 teaspoon ground cinnamon
2 teaspoons freshly grated ginger
1/2 cup (125 ml, 4 fl oz) yoghurt
  or buttermilk
4 tablespoons vegetable oil
4 tablespoons maple syrup
4 tablespoons honey
3 eggs
310 g (10 oz) carrot, grated
makes 12

1 Preheat oven to 200°C (400°F, gas mark 6). In a large bowl combine flour, baking powder, bicarbonate of soda, salt, nutmeg and cinnamon.

2 In a separate bowl, combine ginger, yoghurt, oil, maple syrup, honey and eggs. Add egg mixture to flour mixture and mix to combine. Stir in carrots.

3 Spoon mixture into greased 1/2 cup (125 ml, 4 fl oz) capacity muffin tins. Bake for 15–18 minutes or until muffins are cooked when tested with a skewer. Serve warm.

PREPARATION TIME
20 minutes

COOKING TIME
20 minutes

NUTRITIONAL VALUE PER SERVE   FAT 8.4 G   CARBOHYDRATE 32 G   PROTEIN 4.8 G

Blackberry spice muffins

INGREDIENTS

75 g (2½ oz) self-raising
   wholemeal flour
60 g (2 oz) self-raising flour
½ teaspoon ground allspice
3 tablespoons brown sugar
60 g (2 oz) ground almonds
185 g (6 oz) blackberries
1 banana, mashed
1 cup (250 ml, 8 fl oz) buttermilk
⅓ cup (90 ml, 3 fl oz) vegetable oil
1 egg, lightly beaten
makes 12

PREPARATION TIME
15 minutes

COOKING TIME
25 minutes

1 Preheat oven to 190°C (375°F, gas mark 5). Into a large bowl, sift wholemeal
flour, flour and allspice. Return husks to bowl. Add sugar, almonds,
blackberries and banana and mix to combine.

2 In a large bowl, place buttermilk, oil and egg and whisk to combine. Stir milk
mixture into flour mixture and mix until just combined.

3 Spoon mixture into 12 greased ½ cup (125 ml, 4 fl oz) capacity muffin tins and
bake for 15–20 minutes or until muffins are cooked when tested with a
skewer. Turn onto a wire rack to cool.

NUTRITIONAL VALUE PER SERVE   FAT **14.7** G   CARBOHYDRATE **19** G   PROTEIN **5.1** G

Lemon-currant muffins

INGREDIENTS

2 teaspoons finely grated
   lemon rind (zest)
95 g (3 oz) brown sugar
250 g (8 oz) unbleached plain flour
4 tablespoons raw sugar
1 tablespoon baking powder
1/2 teaspoon salt
1/8 teaspoon ground nutmeg
4 tablespoons dried currants
1 egg
1 cup (250 ml, 8 fl oz) milk
3 tablespoons butter, melted
1 tablespoon finely grated
   lemon rind
1 tablespoon lemon juice
makes 12

PREPARATION TIME
20 minutes

COOKING TIME
25 minutes

1 Preheat oven to 200°C (400°F, gas mark 6). In a small bowl, combine 2 teaspoons lemon rind and brown sugar. Mix well and set aside.

2 In a large bowl, combine flour, raw sugar, baking powder, salt, nutmeg and currants. Make a well in the centre. In a medium bowl, beat the egg. Add milk, butter, lemon juice and remaining lemon rind. Pour egg mixture into flour mixture, stirring until just combined.

3 Pour mixture into 12 greased 1/2 cup (125 ml, 4 fl oz) capacity muffin tins. Sprinkle evenly with lemon sugar and bake 20–25 minutes until muffins are cooked when tested with a skewer. Turn onto wire racks to cool.

NUTRITIONAL VALUE PER SERVE	FAT 7.5 G	CARBOHYDRATE 44 G	PROTEIN 5.1 G

Scones

INGREDIENTS

250 g (8 oz) self-raising flour
1 teaspoon baking powder
2 teaspoons sugar
3 tablespoons butter
1 egg
½ cup (125 ml, 4 fl oz) milk
makes 12

1 Preheat oven to 220°C (425°F, gas mark 7).
Into a large bowl, sift flour and baking powder. Stir in sugar, then rub in butter, using fingertips, until mixture resembles coarse breadcrumbs.

2 In a small bowl, whisk egg and milk. Make a well in the centre of flour mixture, pour in egg mixture and mix to form a soft dough. Turn onto a lightly floured surface and knead lightly.

3 Press dough out to a 2 cm thickness, using palm of hand. Cut out scones using a floured 5 cm pastry cutter. Avoid twisting the cutter or the scones will rise unevenly.

4 Arrange scones close together on a greased and lightly floured baking tray or in a shallow 20 cm round cake tin. Brush with a little milk and bake for 12–15 minutes or until risen and golden.

PREPARATION TIME
15 minutes

COOKING TIME
12–15 minutes

NUTRITIONAL VALUE PER SERVE	FAT 11.8 G	CARBOHYDRATE 38 G	PROTEIN 7.1 G

Fresh strawberry scones

INGREDIENTS

225 g (7½ oz) self-raising
  wholemeal flour
1 teaspoon baking powder
pinch of salt
4 tablespoons butter
2 tablespoons castor sugar
100 g (3½ oz) fresh strawberries,
  chopped
½ cup (125 ml, 4 fl oz) low-fat milk
extra milk for glazing
makes 12

1 Preheat oven to 220°C (425°F, gas mark 7).
   In a large bowl, place flour, baking powder
   and salt and mix to combine. Lightly rub in
   the butter with fingertips until the mixture
   resembles breadcrumbs.

2 Add sugar, strawberries and enough milk to
   form a soft dough. Turn the dough out onto a
   floured surface, knead lightly, then carefully
   roll to a thickness of 2 cm.

3 Cut out 12 rounds, using a 5 cm pastry cutter,
   and place side by side on a baking sheet. Brush
   with milk to glaze. Bake for 8–10 minutes, until
   risen and golden brown. Transfer to a wire rack
   to cool.

PREPARATION TIME
15 minutes

COOKING TIME
10–15 minutes

NUTRITIONAL VALUE PER SERVE	FAT **12.2** G	CARBOHYDRATE **32** G	PROTEIN **6.1** G

Pumpkin scones

INGREDIENTS

4 tablespoons butter
2 tablespoons castor sugar
125 g (4 oz) pumpkin,
  cooked and mashed
¼ teaspoon nutmeg
1 egg
½ cup (125 ml, 4 fl oz) milk
285 g (9 oz) self-raising flour, sifted
makes 12

PREPARATION TIME
15 minutes

COOKING TIME
20 minutes

1 Preheat oven to 210°C (415°F , gas mark 6–7). In a large bowl,
   cream butter and sugar until well combined. Add pumpkin and
   nutmeg and mix well. Add egg, then gradually add milk. Stir in
   sifted flour and gently mix to a soft dough.

2 Turn dough onto a floured surface and knead lightly, then
   carefully roll to a thickness of 2½ cm. Cut out 12 rounds using a
   5 cm pastry cutter.

3 Place onto a greased baking sheet and brush with milk glaze. Bake
   for 15–20 minutes until risen and golden brown. Transfer to a wire
   rack to cool. Serve with butter.

NUTRITIONAL VALUE PER SERVE	FAT 10.9 G	CARBOHYDRATE 34 G	PROTEIN 5.7 G

Cheddar and apple scones

INGREDIENTS

4 tablespoons butter, cubed,
extra butter for greasing
210 g (7 oz) self-raising flour
1 teaspoon baking powder
salt
60 g (2 oz) fine oatmeal
extra oatmeal for dusting
1 teaspoon English mustard powder
1 teaspoon light muscovado sugar
125 g (4 oz) cheddar, cubed
1 large eating apple, peeled, cored
  and chopped into pieces
4–5 tablespoons sour cream
  or buttermilk
extra sour cream or buttermilk
  for glazing
makes 10–12

1 Preheat oven to 200°C (400°F, gas mark 6).
   Grease a large baking sheet.

2 Into a large bowl, sift the flour, baking powder
   and a good pinch of salt, stir in oatmeal,
   mustard powder and sugar. Rub in the butter
   using your fingertips until it resembles fine
   breadcrumbs. Fold in the cheese and apples
   and add just enough sour cream or buttermilk
   to make a soft but not sticky dough.

3 Turn dough out onto a floured surface and
   lightly roll to a thickness of 2 cm and cut out
   10–12 scones, using a 6 cm pastry cutter. Place
   on the baking sheet, brush the tops with
   soured cream or buttermilk and lightly dust
   with oatmeal. Bake for 10–12 minutes until well
   risen and golden. Transfer to a wire rack to cool.

PREPARATION TIME
20 minutes

COOKING TIME
15 minutes

NUTRITIONAL VALUE PER SERVE   FAT **18.5** G   CARBOHYDRATE **27** G   PROTEIN **7.6** G

Mini savoury croissants

INGREDIENTS

250 g (8 oz) prepared puff pastry
1 egg
1 tablespoon water
butter for greasing
asparagus and cheese filling
60 g (2 oz) gruyère cheese, grated
4 fresh asparagus spears,
   blanched and finely chopped
¼ teaspoon ground paprika
black pepper
makes 12

PREPARATION TIME
20 minutes

COOKING TIME
15–20 minutes

1 Preheat oven to 200°C (400°F, gas mark 5). In a large bowl, combine
   cheese, asparagus, paprika and black pepper to taste.

2 Roll out pastry to 0.3 cm-thick and cut into 10 cm-wide strips. Cut each
   strip into triangles with 10 cm edge at the base.

3 Place a little filling across the base of each triangle, roll up from the base
   and mould into a croissant shape. In a small bowl, lightly beat egg with
   water then brush over croissant.

4 Place croissants on greased baking trays and bake for 12–15 minutes or
   until puffed and golden. Serve hot or cold.

| NUTRITIONAL VALUE PER SERVE | FAT 19 G | CARBOHYDRATE 21 G | PROTEIN 8.7 G |

Cheese and bacon damper

INGREDIENTS

310 g (10 oz) self-raising flour
3 tablespoons butter
2 teaspoons dried parsley flakes
1 teaspoon chopped fresh chives
250 g (8 oz) mature cheddar, grated
2 rashers cooked bacon,
  finely chopped
1 egg
3/4 cup (185 ml, 6 fl oz) milk
serves 6–8

1 Preheat oven to 180°C (350°F, gas mark 4).
   Into a large bowl, sift flour. Rub in butter using
   your fingertips, until mixture resembles coarse
   breadcrumbs. Stir in parsley, chives, cheese
   and bacon, and mix well to combine.

2 In a separate bowl, combine the egg and milk.
   Stir into flour mixture and mix to a soft dough.
   Turn dough onto a lightly floured board and
   knead lightly.

3 Shape into a cob and cut a deep cross in the
   centre. Place on a sheet of baking paper on an
   oven tray. Bake for 30 minutes or until risen
   and golden.

PREPARATION TIME
20 minutes

COOKING TIME
30–40 minutes

NUTRITIONAL VALUE PER SERVE	FAT 16.9 G	CARBOHYDRATE 24 G	PROTEIN 13.5 G

Blue cheese and walnut damper

INGREDIENTS

310 g (10 oz) self-raising flour, sifted
220 g (7½ oz) blue cheese, crumbled
1 tablespoon snipped fresh chives
1 teaspoon paprika
155 g (5 oz) walnuts, chopped
1 cup (250 ml, 8 fl oz) buttermilk
  or milk
1 tablespoon walnut or vegetable oil
60 g (2 oz) parmesan, grated
makes 1

1 Preheat oven to 180°C (350°F, gas mark 4).
  In a large bowl, combine flour, blue cheese,
  chives, paprika and 125 g (4 oz) walnuts.

2 Make a well in the centre of flour mixture,
  add milk and oil and mix to form a soft dough.

3 Turn dough onto a lightly floured surface and
  knead until smooth. Roll into a large ball,
  flatten slightly and place on a lightly greased
  baking tray. Sprinkle with parmesan and
  remaining walnuts. Bake for 40 minutes or
  until golden and risen.

PREPARATION TIME
20 minutes

COOKING TIME
40 minutes

NUTRITIONAL VALUE PER SERVE	FAT 22.4 G	CARBOHYDRATE 22 G	PROTEIN 12.6 G

Sun-dried tomato and provolone quick bread

INGREDIENTS

4 tablespoons olive oil
2 tablespoons sugar
2 large eggs
2 cloves garlic, crushed
1¼ cups (185 ml, 6 fl oz) buttermilk
375 g (12 oz) unbleached bread flour
2 teaspoon baking powder
½ teaspoon bicarbonate of soda
1½ teaspoons salt
125 g (4 oz) provolone or other
   sharp yellow cheese, grated
60 g (2 oz) spring onions
   (green onions), thinly sliced
30 g (1 oz) fresh parsley, chopped
1 teaspoon freshly ground
   black pepper
80 g (3 oz) sun-dried tomatoes,
   chopped
serves 4–6

PREPARATION TIME
25 minutes

COOKING TIME
50 minutes

1 In a large bowl, combine the oil, sugar, eggs, garlic and buttermilk until smooth.

2 In a separate bowl, combine the flour, baking powder, bicarbonate of soda and salt, then add cheese, spring onions, parsley, pepper and tomatoes.

3 Add the buttermilk mixture to the flour mixture and stir until just combined.

4 Pour the batter into a greased 20 cm x 10 cm loaf tin, smooth top with a wet spoon and bake for 50 minutes or until risen and golden. Allow to cool for 10 minutes before removing from tin.

NUTRITIONAL VALUE PER SERVE	FAT 12.4 G	CARBOHYDRATE 31 G	PROTEIN 9.7 G

Olive soda bread

INGREDIENTS

125 g (4 oz) butter, softened
4 tablespoons sugar
1 egg
450 g (14 oz) wholemeal
   self-raising flour
185 g (6 oz) plain flour
1½ teaspoons bicarbonate of soda
1½ cups (375 ml, 12 fl oz)
   buttermilk or milk
125 g (4 oz) pitted black olives,
   chopped
2 teaspoons dried fennel seeds
1 teaspoon coarse sea salt
makes 1

PREPARATION TIME
20 minutes

COOKING TIME
45 minutes

1 Preheat oven to 200°C (400°F, gas mark 6). In a food processor,
   place butter, sugar and egg and process until smooth. Add
   wholemeal flour, plain flour, bicarbonate of soda and milk and
   process to form a soft dough.

2 Turn dough onto a lightly floured surface and knead in olives.
   Shape dough into a 20 cm round and place on a lightly greased
   and floured baking tray.

3 Using a sharp knife, cut a cross in the top. Sprinkle with fennel
   seeds and salt and bake for 45 minutes or until golden and firm.

NUTRITIONAL VALUE PER SERVE   FAT **9.9** G   CARBOHYDRATE **37** G   PROTEIN **6.8** G

Blueberry pecan loaf

INGREDIENTS

250 g (8 oz) unbleached plain flour
2 teaspoon baking powder
½ teaspoon salt
¼ teaspoon bicarbonate of soda
¼ teaspoon ground nutmeg
125 g (4 oz) sugar
60 g (2 oz) pecans, chopped
2 eggs
4 tablespoons milk
½ cup (125 ml, 4 fl oz) orange juice
2 teaspoons grated orange
   rind (zest)
90 g (3 oz) butter, melted
155 g (5 oz) blueberries
makes 1

PREPARATION TIME
25 minutes

COOKING TIME
65–70 minutes

1 Preheat oven to 180°C (350°F, gas mark 4). In a large bowl combine
   flour, baking powder, salt, bicarbonate of soda, nutmeg and sugar.
   Mix in pecans. Make a well in the centre.

2 In a medium bowl, beat eggs with milk, orange juice and rind. Fold
   in melted butter. Add egg mixture to flour mixture, mixing until
   just combined. Gently fold in blueberries.

3 Pour batter into a well-greased 20 x 10 cm loaf tin. Bake for 55–65
   minutes until loaf is golden and risen. Cool in pan for 10 minutes.
   Turn onto a wire rack to cool.

NUTRITIONAL VALUE PER SERVE	FAT 13.2 G	CARBOHYDRATE 33 G	PROTEIN 5 G

Hot-cross buns

INGREDIENTS

60 g (2 oz) skim milk powder
1 cup (250 ml, 8 fl oz) warm water
75 g (2½ oz) sugar
90 g (3 oz) butter, melted
2 tablespoons dried yeast
500 g (1 lb) plain flour
1 teaspoon salt
1 teaspoon ground cinnamon
1 teaspoon mixed spice
1 tablespoon gluten powder
5 tablespoons currants
4 tablespoons sultanas
1 tablespoon mixed peel
cross batter
3 tablespoons plain flour
3 teaspoons castor sugar
water to mix
bun glaze
½ cup (125 ml, 4 fl oz) water
125 g (4 oz) sugar
makes 16

1 Preheat oven to 230°C (450°F, gas mark 8). In a large bowl, dissolve milk powder in warm water. Add ⅓ cup of sugar, butter and yeast. Into another large bowl, sift 4 cups of flour, salt, spices and gluten. Pour the yeast mixture over dry ingredients, mix well to form a soft dough – adding extra warm water if necessary.

2 Knead mixture thoroughly on a floured board for 10 minutes or until smooth.

3 Place dough in a greased bowl, cover with a tea towel and stand in a warm place for about 45 minutes until mixture doubles in size. Knead the currants and sultanas into the dough. Shape the dough into 16 buns and place in a greased deep-sided large baking dish. Stand in a warm place for a further 15–20 minutes.

4 In a bowl, combine flour and castor sugar, adding enough water to give a cream like consistency. Using this batter, pipe crosses on each bun.

5 Bake for 15 minutes or until buns are golden and firm. Place remaining sugar and water in a small saucepan, stir over low heat until sugar has dissolved. Simmer for 5 minutes without stirring. Brush buns with glaze while hot. Transfer onto wire racks to cool.

PREPARATION TIME
1 hour

COOKING TIME
30 minutes

NUTRITIONAL VALUE PER SERVE	FAT 7.8 G	CARBOHYDRATE 68 G	PROTEIN 8.3 G

Apricot banana bread

INGREDIENTS

250 g (8 oz) unbleached plain flour
1 teaspoon baking powder
½ teaspoon bicarbonate of soda
½ teaspoon salt
250 g (8 oz) sugar
125 g (4 oz) dried apricots, chopped
60 g (2 oz) walnuts, chopped
1 egg
½ cup (125 ml, 4 fl oz) milk
1 tablespoon walnut oil
1 tablespoon oil
1 ripe banana, mashed
makes 1

PREPARATION TIME
25 minutes

COOKING TIME
70 minutes

1 Preheat oven to 180°C (350°F, gas mark 4). In a large bowl, combine flour, baking powder, bicarbonate of soda, salt and sugar. Add apricots and walnuts, mix to combine. Make a well in the centre.

2 In a medium bowl, beat the egg with milk and oils. Fold in banana. Add banana mixture to flour mixture, stirring until just combined.

3 Pour batter into a well greased 20 x 10 cm loaf tin. Bake for 65–70 minutes until loaf is well browned. Cool in tin for 10 minutes. Turn onto a wire rack to cool.

NUTRITIONAL VALUE PER SERVE	FAT 9 G	CARBOHYDRATE 50 G	PROTEIN 5.3 G

Glossary

Al dente: Italian term to describe pasta and rice that are cooked until tender but still firm to the bite.

Bake blind: to bake pastry cases without their fillings. Line the raw pastry case with greaseproof paper and fill with raw rice or dried beans to prevent collapsed sides and puffed base. Remove paper and fill 5 minutes before completion of cooking time.

Baste: to spoon hot cooking liquid over food at intervals during cooking to moisten and flavour it.

Beat: to make a mixture smooth with rapid and regular motions using a spatula, wire whisk or electric mixer; to make a mixture light and smooth by enclosing air.

Beurre manié: equal quantities of butter and flour mixed together to a smooth paste and stirred bit by bit into a soup, stew or sauce while on the heat to thicken. Stop adding when desired thickness results.

Bind: to add egg or a thick sauce to hold ingredients together when cooked.

Blanch: to plunge some foods into boiling water for less than a minute and immediately plunge into iced water. This is to brighten the colour of some vegetables; to remove skin from tomatoes and nuts.

Blend: to mix 2 or more ingredients thoroughly together; do not confuse with blending in an electric blender.

Boil: to cook in a liquid brought to boiling point and kept there.

Boiling point: when bubbles rise continually and break over the entire surface of the liquid, reaching a temperature of 100°C (212°F). In some cases food is held at this high temperature for a few seconds then heat is turned to low for slower cooking. See simmer.

Bouquet garni: a bundle of several herbs tied together with string for easy removal, placed into pots of stock, soups and stews for flavour. A few sprigs of fresh thyme, parsley and bay leaf are used. Can be purchased in sachet form for convenience.

Caramelise: to heat sugar in a heavy-based pan until it liquefies and develops a caramel colour. Vegetables such as blanched carrots and sautéed onions may be sprinkled with sugar and caramelised.

Chill: to place in the refrigerator or stir over ice until cold.

Clarify: to make a liquid clear by removing sediments and impurities. To melt fat and remove any sediment.

Coat: to dust or roll food items in flour to cover the surface before the food is cooked. Also, to coat in flour, egg and breadcrumbs.

Cool: to stand at room temperature until some or all heat is removed, e.g. cool a little, cool completely.

Cream: to make creamy and fluffy by working the mixture with the back of a wooden spoon, usually refers to creaming butter and sugar or margarine. May also be creamed with an electric mixer.

Croutons: small cubes of bread, toasted or fried, used as an addition to salads or as a garnish to soups and stews.

Crudite: raw vegetable sticks served with a dipping sauce.

Crumb: to coat foods in flour, egg and breadcrumbs to form a protective coating for foods which are fried. Also adds flavour, texture and enhances appearance.

Cube: to cut into small pieces with six even sides, e.g. cubes of meat.

Cut in: to combine fat and flour using 2 knives scissor fashion or with a pastry blender, to make pastry.

Deglaze: to dissolve dried out cooking juices left on the base and sides of a roasting dish or frying pan. Add a little water, wine or stock, scrape and stir over heat until dissolved. Resulting liquid is used to make a flavoursome gravy or added to a sauce or casserole.

Degrease: to skim fat from the surface of cooking liquids, e.g. stocks, soups, casseroles.

Dice: to cut into small cubes.

Dredge: to heavily coat with icing sugar, sugar, flour or cornflour.

Dressing: a mixture added to completed dishes to add moisture and flavour, e.g. salads, cooked vegetables.

Drizzle: to pour in a fine thread-like stream moving over a surface.

Egg wash: beaten egg with milk or water used to brush over pastry, bread dough or biscuits to give a sheen and golden brown colour.

Essence: a strong flavouring liquid, usually made by distillation. Only a few drops are needed to flavour.

Fillet: a piece of prime meat, fish or poultry which is boneless or has all bones removed.

Flake: to separate cooked fish into flakes, removing any bones and skin, using 2 forks.

Flame: to ignite warmed alcohol over food or to pour into a pan with food, ignite then serve.

Flute: to make decorative indentations around the pastry rim before baking.

Fold in: combining of a light, whisked or creamed mixture with other ingredients. Add a portion of the other ingredients at a time and mix using a gentle circular motion, over and under the mixture so that air will not be lost. Use a silver spoon or spatula.

Glaze: to brush or coat food with a liquid that will give the finished product a glossy appearance, and on baked products, a golden brown colour.

Grease: to rub the surface of a metal or heatproof dish with oil or fat, to prevent the food from sticking.

Herbed butter: softened butter mixed with finely chopped fresh herbs and re-chilled. Used to serve on grilled meats and fish.

Hors D'Oeuvre: small savoury foods served as an appetiser, popularly known today as 'finger food'.

Infuse: to steep foods in a liquid until the liquid absorbs their flavour.

Joint: to cut poultry and game into serving pieces by dividing at the joint.

Julienne: to cut some food, e.g. vegetables and processed meats into fine strips the length of matchsticks. Used for inclusion in salads or as a garnish to cooked dishes.

Knead: to work a yeast dough in a pressing, stretching and folding motion with the heel of the hand until smooth and elastic to develop the gluten strands. Non-yeast doughs should be lightly and quickly handled as gluten development is not desired.

Line: to cover the inside of a baking tin with paper for the easy removal of the cooked product from the baking tin.

Macerate: to stand fruit in a syrup, liqueur or spirit to give added flavour.

Marinade: a flavoured liquid, into which food is placed for some time to give it flavour and to tenderise. Marinades include an acid ingredient such as vinegar or wine, oil and seasonings.

Mask: to evenly cover cooked food portions with a sauce, mayonnaise or savoury jelly.

Pan-fry: to fry foods in a small amount of fat or oil, sufficient to coat the base of the pan.

Parboil: to boil until partially cooked. The food is then finished by some other method.

Pare: to peel the skin from vegetables and fruit. Peel is the popular term but pare is the name given to the knife used; paring knife.

Pith: the white lining between the rind and flesh of oranges, grapefruit and lemons.

Pit: to remove stones or seeds from olives, cherries, dates.

Pitted: the olives, cherries, dates etc. with the stone removed, e.g. purchase pitted dates.

Poach: to simmer gently in enough hot liquid to almost cover the food so shape will be retained.

Pound: to flatten meats with a meat mallet; to reduce to a paste or small particles with a mortar and pestle.

Simmer: to cook in liquid just below boiling point at about 96°C (205°F) with small bubbles rising gently to the surface.

Skim: to remove fat or froth from the surface of simmering food.

Stock: the liquid produced when meat, poultry, fish or vegetables have been simmered in water to extract the flavour. Used as a base for soups, sauces, casseroles etc. Convenience stock products are available.

Sweat: to cook sliced onions or vegetables, in a small amount of butter in a covered pan over low heat, to soften them and release flavour without colouring.

Conversions

Measurements differ from country to country, so it's important to understand what the differences are. This Measurements Guide gives you simple 'at-a-glance' information for using the recipes in this book, wherever you may be.

Cooking is not an exact science – minor variations in measurements won't make a difference to your cooking.

EQUIPMENT

There is a difference in the size of measuring cups used internationally, but the difference is minimal (only 2–3 teaspoons). We use the Australian standard metric measurements in our recipes:

1 teaspoon ....5 ml	1 tablespoon....20 ml
1/2 cup......125 ml	1 cup.....250 ml
4 cups...1 litre	

Measuring cups come in sets of one cup (250 ml), 1/2 cup (125 ml), 1/3 cup (80 ml) and 1/4 cup (60 ml). Use these for measuring liquids and certain dry ingredients.

Measuring spoons come in a set of four and should be used for measuring dry and liquid ingredients.

When using cup or spoon measures always make them level (unless the recipe indicates otherwise).

DRY VERSUS WET INGREDIENTS

While this system of measures is consistent for liquids, it's more difficult to quantify dry ingredients. For instance, one level cup equals: 200 g of brown sugar; 210 g of castor sugar; and 110 g of icing sugar.

When measuring dry ingredients such as flour, don't push the flour down or shake it into the cup. It is best just to spoon the flour in until it reaches the desired amount. When measuring liquids use a clear vessel indicating metric levels.

Always use medium eggs (55–60 g) when eggs are required in a recipe.

OVEN

Your oven should always be at the right temperature before placing the food in it to be cooked. Note that if your oven doesn't have a fan you may need to cook food for a little longer.

MICROWAVE

It is difficult to give an exact cooking time for microwave cooking. It is best to watch what you are cooking closely to monitor its progress.

STANDING TIME

Many foods continue to cook when you take them out of the oven or microwave. If a recipe states that the food needs to 'stand' after cooking, be sure not to overcook the dish.

CAN SIZES

The can sizes available in your supermarket or grocery store may not be the same as specified in the recipe. Don't worry if there is a small variation in size – it's unlikely to make a difference to the end result.

dry		liquids	
metric (grams)	imperial (ounces)	metric (millilitres)	imperial (fluid ounces)
		30 ml	1 fl oz
30 g	1 oz	60 ml	2 fl oz
60 g	2 oz	90 ml	3 fl oz
90 g	3 oz	100 ml	3 ½ fl oz
100 g	3 ½ oz	125 ml	4 fl oz
125 g	4 oz	150 ml	5 fl oz
150 g	5 oz	190 ml	6 fl oz
185 g	6 oz	250 ml	8 fl oz
200 g	7 oz	300 ml	10 fl oz
250 g	8 oz	500 ml	16 fl oz
280 g	9 oz	600 ml	20 fl oz (1 pint)*
315 g	10 oz	1000 ml (1 litre)	32 fl oz
330 g	11 oz		
370 g	12 oz		
400 g	13 oz		
440 g	14 oz		
470 g	15 oz		
500 g	16 oz (1 lb)		
750 g	24 oz (1 ½ lb)		
1000 g (1 kg)	32 oz (2 lb)		*Note: an American pint is 16 fl oz.

cooking temperatures	°C (celsius)	°F (fahrenheit)	gas mark
very slow	120	250	½
slow	150	300	2
moderately slow	160	315	2–3
moderate	180	350	4
moderate hot	190	375	5
	200	400	6
hot	220	425	7
very hot	230	450	8
	240	475	9
	250	500	10

Index

Essential COOKING SERIES

COMPREHENSIVE, STEP BY STEP COOKING

Essential COOKING SERIES
COMPREHENSIVE, STEP BY STEP COOKING
Baking

Essential COOKING SERIES
COMPREHENSIVE, STEP BY STEP COOKING
Chicken Meals

Essential COOKING SERIES
COMPREHENSIVE, STEP BY STEP COOKING
Salads & Greens

Essential COOKING SERIES
COMPREHENSIVE, STEP BY STEP COOKING
Soups & Hors D'Oeuvres

Essential COOKING SERIES
COMPREHENSIVE, STEP BY STEP COOKING
Meat Dishes

Essential COOKING SERIES
COMPREHENSIVE, STEP BY STEP COOKING
Finger Food

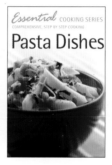

Essential COOKING SERIES
COMPREHENSIVE, STEP BY STEP COOKING
Pasta Dishes

Essential COOKING SERIES
COMPREHENSIVE, STEP BY STEP COOKING
Grilling & Barbecuing

Essential COOKING SERIES
COMPREHENSIVE, STEP BY STEP COOKING
Rice & Risotto

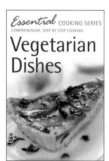

Essential COOKING SERIES
COMPREHENSIVE, STEP BY STEP COOKING
Vegetarian Dishes

Essential COOKING SERIES
COMPREHENSIVE, STEP BY STEP COOKING
Asian Dishes

Essential COOKING SERIES
COMPREHENSIVE, STEP BY STEP COOKING
Stir-Fry